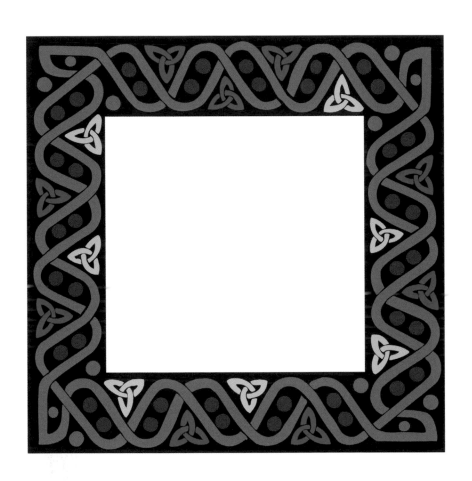

BORDERS AND FRAMES

BORDERS AND FRAMES

DOVERPICTURA

DOVER PUBLICATIONS, INC. | Mineola, New York

Selected and designed by Althea Chen, Faith Brosnan, and Alan Weller.

Borders and Frames is a new work, first published by Dover Publications, Inc., in 2007.

For permission to use more than ten images, please contact:
Permissions Department
Dover Publications, Inc.
31 East 2nd Street
Mineola, NY 11501
rights@doverpublications.com

The CD-ROM file names correspond to the images in the book. All of the artwork stored on the CD-ROM can be imported directly into a wide range of design and word-processing programs on either Windows or Macintosh platforms. No further installation is necessary.

ISBN 10: 0-486-99847-9
ISBN 13: 978-0-486-99847-3

Manufactured in the United States of America
Dover Publications, Inc., 31 East 2nd Street, Mineola, NY 11501
www.doverpublications.com

005

006

8

007

008

010

011

012

013

014

015

012

016

017

018

019

020

14

021

022

15

023

16

025

027

030

031

029

22

032

033

034

035

036

037

038

26

039

040

041

042

043

044

045

046

047

048

050

051

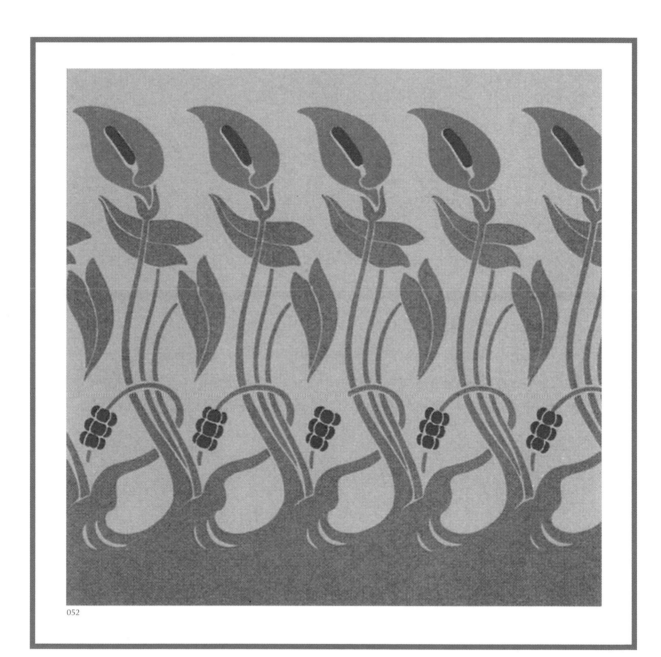

052

054

055

056

057

058

059

060

061

062

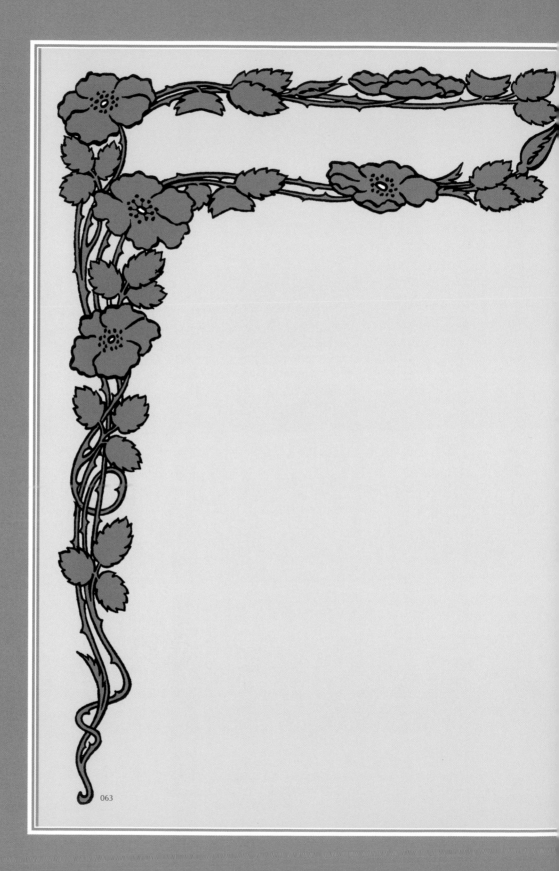

063

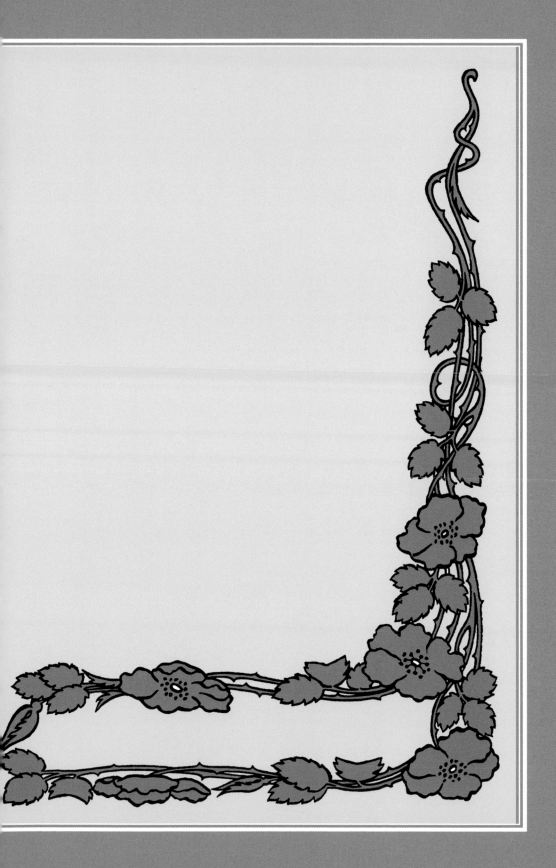

064

065

066

067

068

069

070

071

072

073

074

075

076

077

078

079

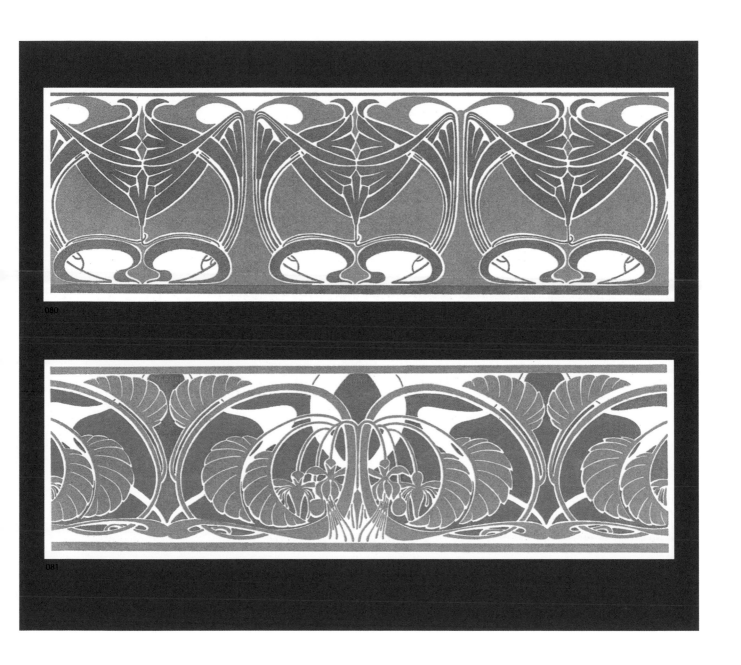

080

081

54

082

083

084

085

086

087

088

089

090

091

092

093

094

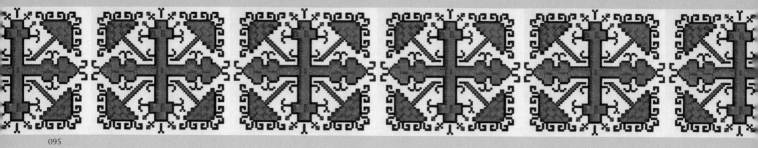

095

096

097

098

099

60

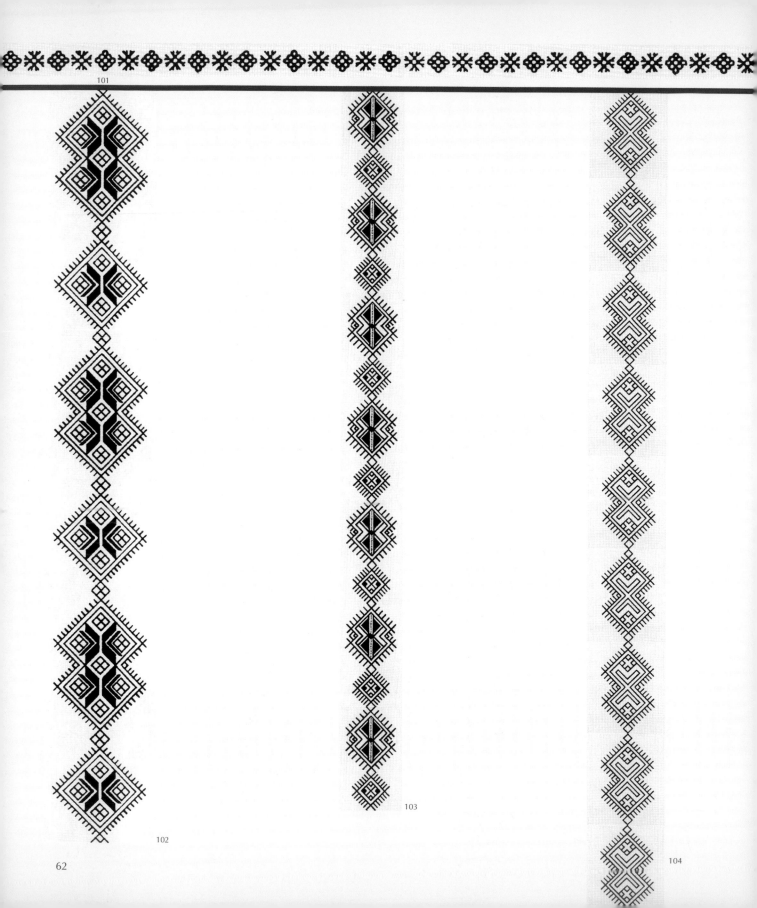

101

102

103

104

105

106

107

108

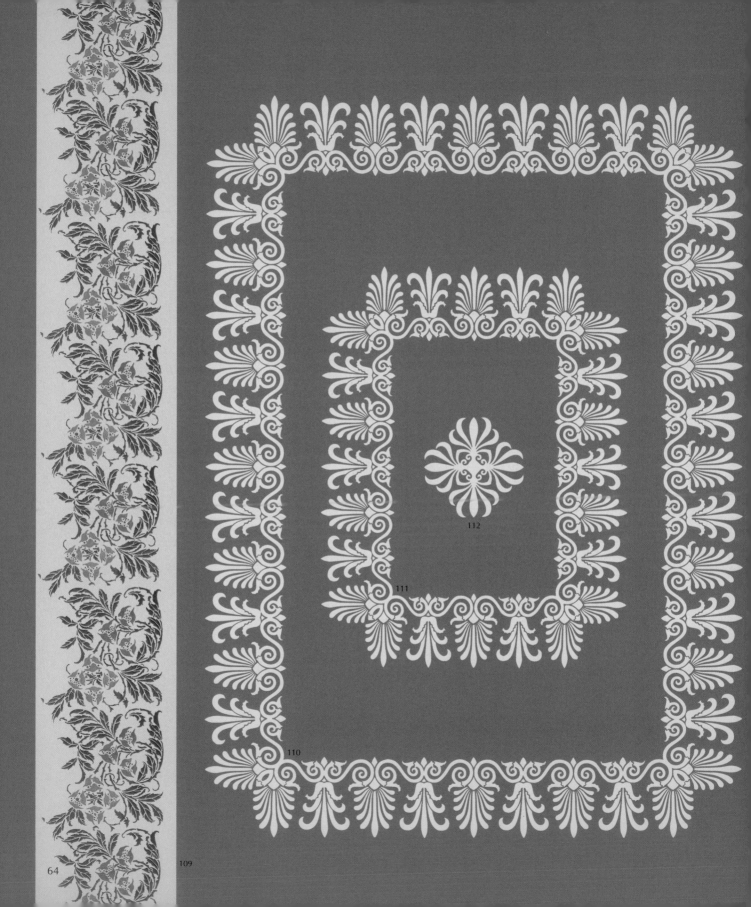

64

109

110

111

112

113

114

115

116

117

119

118

120

121

122

123

124

125

126

127

128

129

130

131

132

133

134

135

136

137

138

139

140

141

142

143

144

145

146

147

148

149

150

151

152

153

154

155

157

158

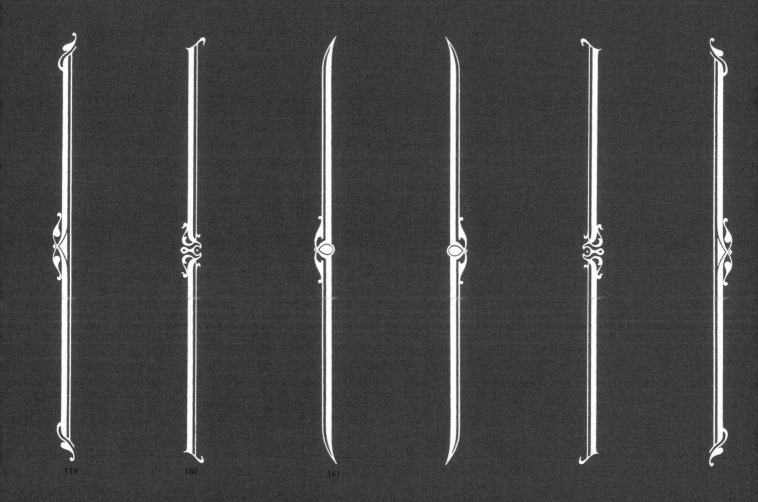

159   160   161

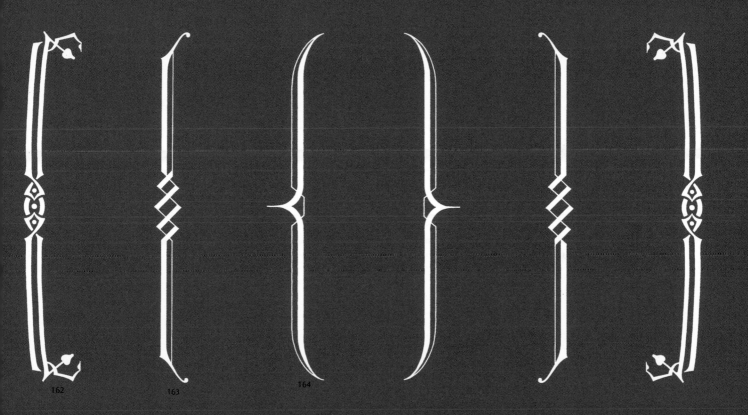

162   163   164

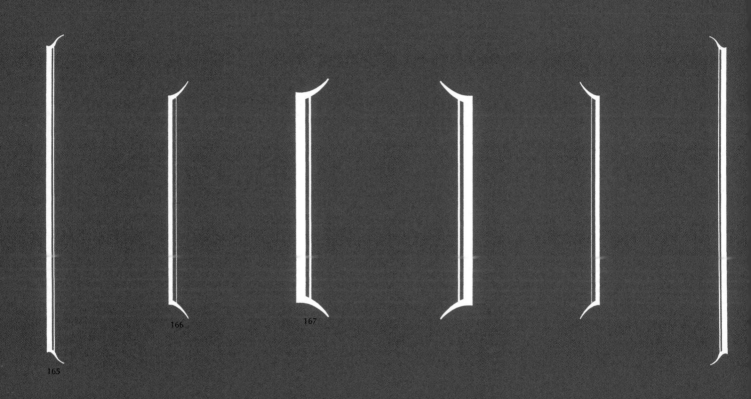

165 166 167

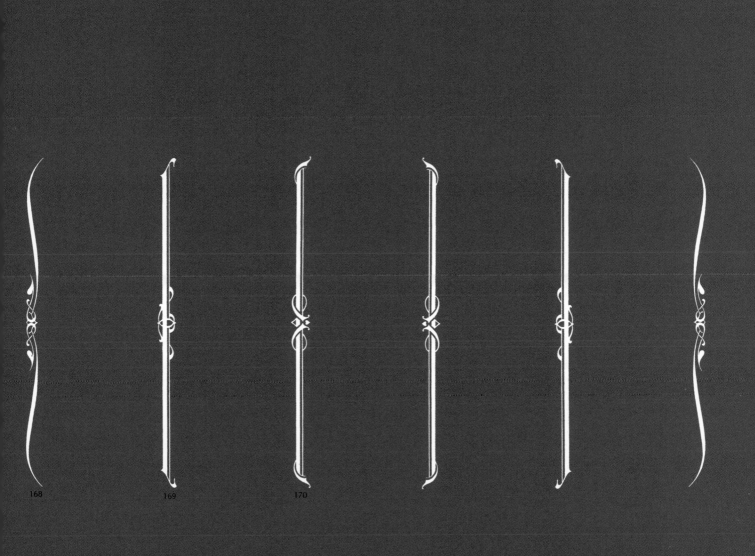

168

169

170

171

172

173

174

175

176

177

178

180

181

182

183

184

185

186

187

188

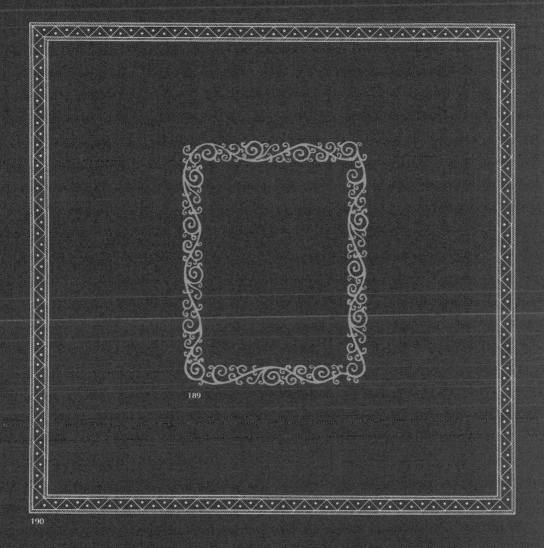

189

190

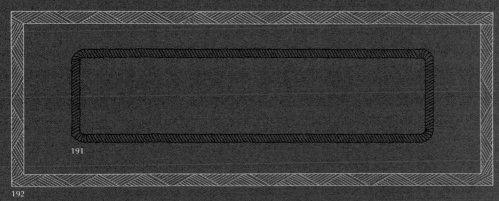

191

192

193

197

196

195

194

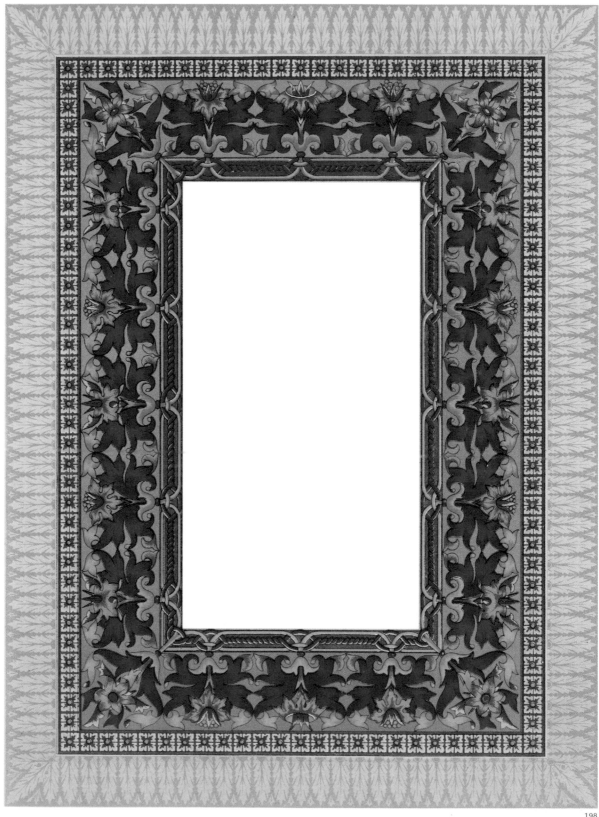

198

199

201

204

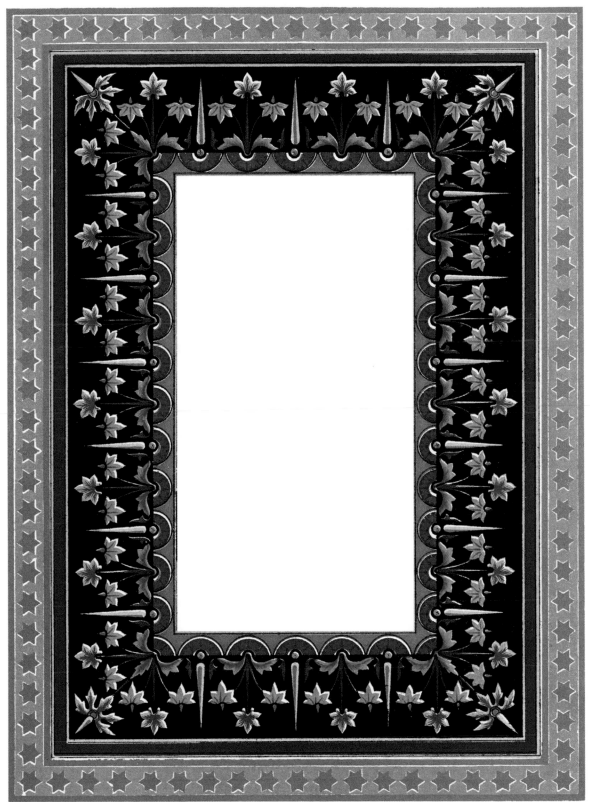

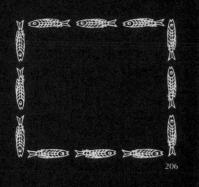

206

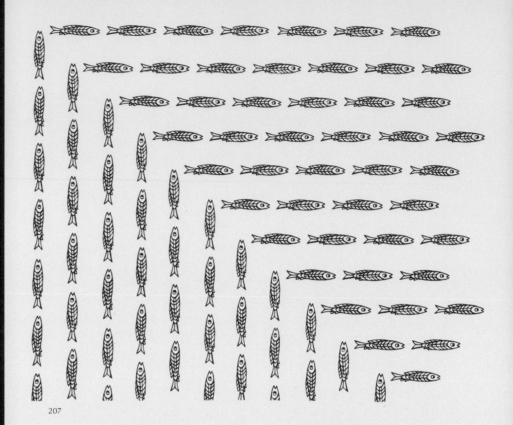

207

208

209

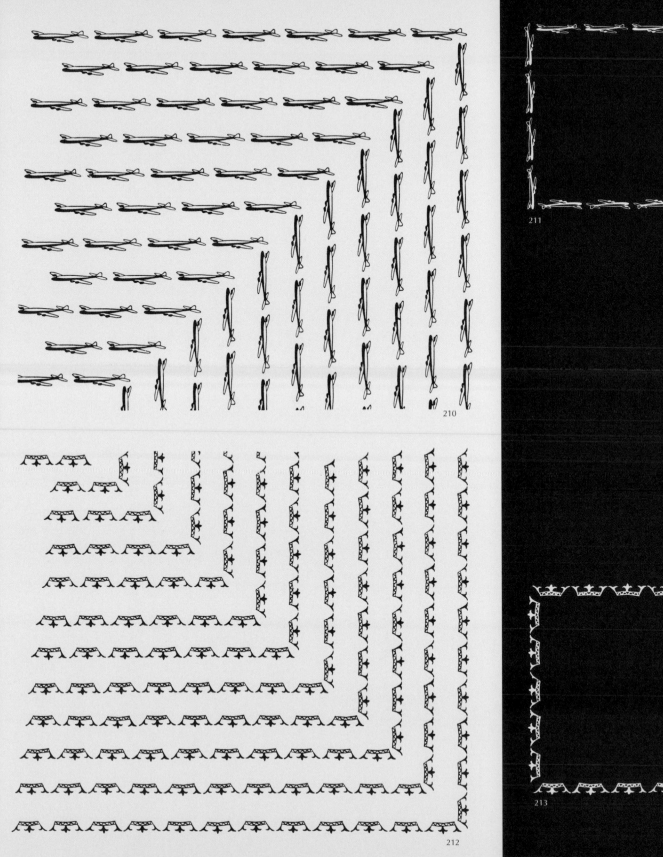

210

211

212

213

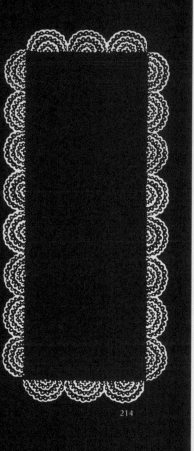

214

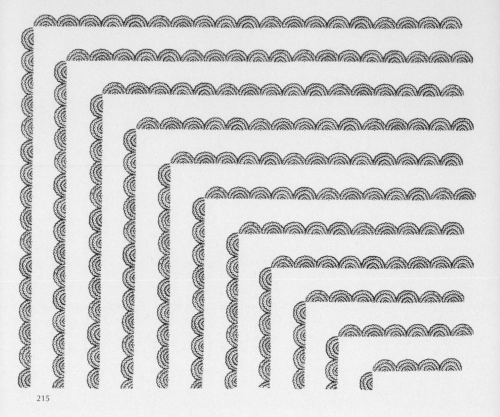

215

216

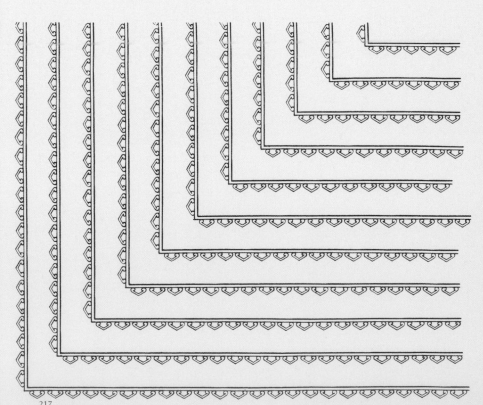

217

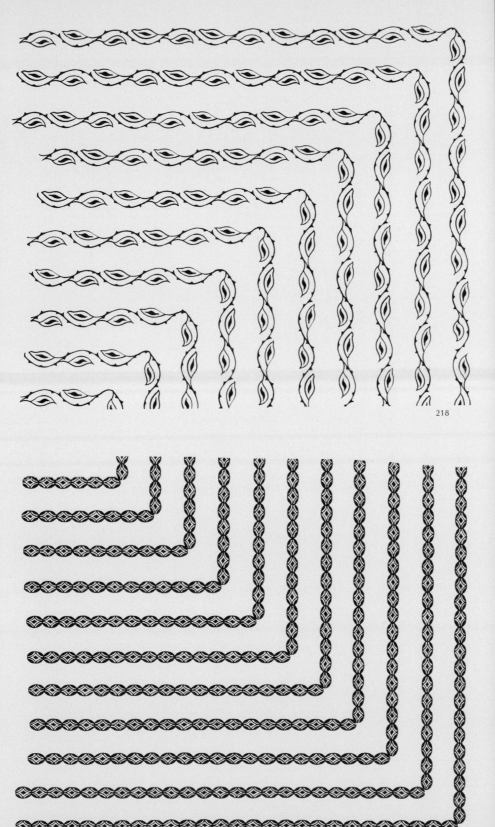

218

220

219

221

222

223

224

225

226

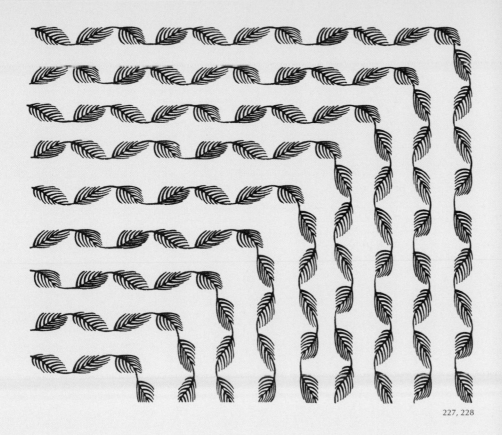

227, 228

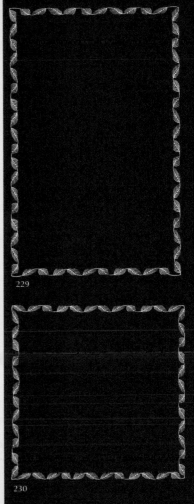

229

230

232

231

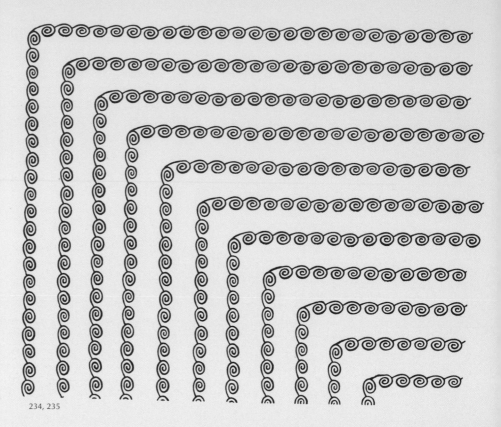

233

234, 235

236

237, 238

239

240

241

242

243

244

247

246

248

249

250

251

252

253

254

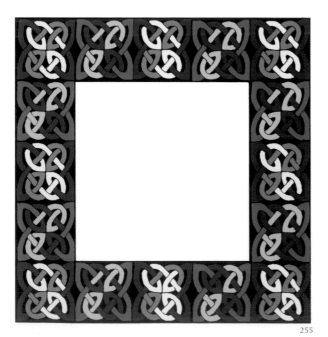

255

256

257

258

259

List of Vector Images

013	128	159	187	223
018	129	160	188	224
034	130	161	189	225
036	131	162	190	226
038	132	163	191	227
040	133	164	192	228
042	134	165	193	229
044	135	166	194	230
046	136	167	195	231
048	137	168	196	232
049	138	169	197	233
110	140	170	206	234
111	141	171	207	235
112	142	172	208	236
113	143	173	209	237
114	145	174	210	238
115	147	175	211	239
117	148	176	212	240
118	149	177	213	241
119	150	178	214	242
120	151	179	215	243
121	152	180	216	
122	153	181	217	
123	154	182	218	
124	155	183	219	
125	156	184	220	
126	157	185	221	
127	158	186	222	